THE
SPECIAL EDUCATOR'S
Calendar and Planning Journal

Motivation, Inspiration, and Affirmation

Mary Zabolio McGrath

Beverley Holden Johns

Skyhorse Publishing

Skyhorse Publishing books may be purchased in bulk at special discounts for sales promotion, corporate gifts, fund-raising, or educational purposes. Special editions can also be created to specifications. For details, contact the Special Sales Department, Skyhorse Publishing, 307 West 36th Street, 11th Floor, New York, NY 10018 or info@skyhorsepublishing.com.

Skyhorse® and Skyhorse Publishing® are registered trademarks of Skyhorse Publishing, Inc.®, a Delaware corporation.

www.skyhorsepublishing.com

10 9 8 7 6 5 4 3 2 1

Library of Congress Cataloging-in-Publication Data is available on file.

ISBN: 978-1-62914-251-7

Printed in China

Acquisitions Editor:	Carol Chambers Collins
Editorial Assistant:	Brett Ory
Production Editor:	Appingo Publishing Services
Cover Designer:	Audrey Snodgrass
Graphic Designer:	Scott Van Atta

Contents

Preface

Special educators wear many hats and must be lifelong learners to be effective in their many roles. This calendar has been designed to provide you with some practical suggestions as you work to meet the needs of students with disabilities.

Because both of us, as authors of *The Special Educator's Calendar and Planning Journal,* come from an extensive background in special education, we aim to compile our experiences and present them to you, the reader, in a concentrated form. By selecting a specific theme each month, we invite you to focus with us on important topics that determine the success of any special educator. By doing so we offer other ideas to apply to your work setting through our daily reminders.

As we partner with you through a twelve-month cycle, we suggest that you note on the space available for each day a response to the thought of the day or a personal reflection based on what you noted in your job setting, an idea you wish to try, or a frustration you experienced. We also encourage you to take time to think about ways to apply the ideas from your reflection as you grow in your role as a special educator.

Take time to go back over your reflections and our offerings as you review in your mind the events of your day, week, and month. Place on your calendar time for brief or extended reflection to secure benefit for your students, families, and certainly for yourself. Be ready to add anything you believe to be your next step to the goals list provided. Check off when you have accomplished this. Include comments on how your situation was impacted by inclusion of this goal.

Special educators must, of necessity, be deadline oriented. Also note the space available for listing important deadlines. This includes IEP due dates and important meeting and conference dates. Though you may have these noted in your files or on a desk or district calendar, we recommend that you list them here as well so that you can see them in the context of the daily input we offer, as well as your plans gleaned from consistent daily reflection. It is by doing this that you will then bring the dimension of your reflection into your professional planning, meetings, and experiences with others.

Once you have begun the routine of reading an idea and reflecting on it, as well as on your teaching day, on a regular basis we ask you to consider how this will bring a broader scope to your work. Being in the habit of observing, noting, and reflecting, you may then respond to your professional reading, conferences, district meetings, and other experiences in a mode of alertness for material for reflection and, consequently, insightful, reflective time leading to strategic application.

ACKNOWLEDGMENTS

We gratefully acknowledge the contributions of the following reviewers:

Sharonjoy A. Jackson
President-Elect, Illinois Council for Exceptional Children
Past President, CEC Pioneers Division

Beverly Levitt
Special Education Teacher
Round Lake School District 116, IL

Mary Beth Schafer
Special Education Consultant
Elk River, MN

About the Authors

 **Mary Zabolio McGrath** taught in Bloomington, Minnesota, public schools for thirty-one years, working as a classroom teacher, a demonstration teacher with the Project Read program, and a special education teacher in learning disabilities, behavior disorders, and developmental delay. She has served as national secretary for the Council for Behavior Disorders and on the board of the Minnesota Council for Exceptional Children.

Mary has a doctorate from the University of Minnesota in educational administration, with collateral work in organizational communication. She earned a master's degree in educational psychology.

Mary has written articles for educators, parents, caregivers, and the general public, several of which are posted on her Web site, www.maryzmcgrath.com. In addition, she has authored/coauthored books on educational subjects.

Currently Mary works as a professional speaker, working with schools, parents, and organizations to reflect on and improve the quality of career relationships and life transitions. She is a member of the National Speakers Association and Toastmasters International.

 **Beverley Holden Johns** supervised LD and EBD teachers in twenty-two school districts and was the founder and administrator of the Garrison Alternative School for students with severe EBD in Jacksonville, Illinois, and later the coordinator for staff development for the Four Rivers Special Education District. She is now a learning and behavior consultant and an adjunct instructor for MacMurray College, where she teaches the course on special education law, on adaptations for the general education classroom, and on EBD.

She chaired the Tenth Biennial Conference of the International Association of Special Education (IASE) held June 10 to 14, 2007, in Hong Kong and has served as president of IASE (www.iase.org). She presented the Inaugural Marden Lecture at The University of Hong Kong in January 2006.

Beverley is the lead author of nine books (and coauthor of two others): *Reduction of School Violence: Alternatives to Suspension*; *Techniques for Managing Verbally and Physically Aggressive Students*; *Surviving Internal Politics Within the School*; *Safe Schools*; *The Teacher's Reflective Calendar and Planning Journal*; *Reaching Students With Diverse Disabilities*; *Effective Curriculum and Instruction for Students With Emotional/Behavioral Disorders*; *Students With Disabilities and General Education: A Desktop Reference for School Personnel*; *Getting Behavioral Interventions Right; Preparing Test-Resistant Students for Assessments: A Staff Training Guide*; and *Ethical Dilemmas in Education.* She has written a workbook to accompany a video for paraprofessionals, titled *The Paraprofessional's Guide to Managing Student Behavior,* and more than forty articles.

She is coauthor with Janet Lerner of the eleventh edition of the seminal college LD textbook of *Learning Disabilities and Related Mild Disabilities.*

She is the 2000 recipient of the CEC Outstanding Leadership Award from the International Council for Exceptional Children, past international president and current board member of the Council for Children with Behavioral Disorders, and the 2007 recipient of the Romaine P. Mackie Leadership Service Award.

She is listed in *Who's Who in America*, *Who's Who of American Women*, *Who's Who in American Education,* and *Who's Who Among America's Teachers*. She has chaired the Illinois Special Education Coalition, whose membership includes thirteen statewide organizations, for 27 years.

She is past president of the Learning Disabilities Association of Illinois and has been the national state president's representative serving on the board of LDA of America.

She has presented workshops across the United States and Canada; in San Juan, Puerto Rico; Sydney, Australia (keynote); Warsaw, Poland; Hong Kong, China; and Lima, Peru.

To special educators who set aside time daily to reflect on the importance of their mission to offer instruction, support, and dignity to children with special needs.

LOOKING AHEAD TO A NEW SCHOOL YEAR

August sends the signal to us that it is time to get ready to go back to school. It is time to get our rooms ready, get our bulletin boards up, review our new class lists, review the materials we have, and plan for an exciting school year. You will feel much better if you have your classroom ready early.

Goals

_____

_____

_____

_____

_____

_____

_____

_____

_____

_____

_____

_____

_____

August

August 1

If you have a new classroom, go to school and decide how you will arrange the room to meet the needs of your students.

_____

_____

_____

_____

August 2

If you have the same classroom, give it a facelift with new plants or lamps.

_____

_____

_____

_____

August 3

Review the materials available to you. Find out whether there is additional money in the budget for ordering new materials.

_____

_____

_____

_____

August 4

Determine and establish your paperwork organizational system for the year.

_____

_____

_____

_____

August 5

Establish a positive recognition system for your students for appropriate behavior.

_____

_____

_____

_____

August 6

Determine your rules for your classroom, and make a poster about them with pictures or photos depicting students following the rules.

_____

_____

_____

_____

August 7

Spend some time with the principal, secretary, and custodian to get to know their expectations for the year.

_____

_____

_____

_____

August 8

Send an introductory letter to your students and their parents.

_____

_____

_____

_____

August 9

Create a bulletin board that focuses on each student.

_____

_____

_____

_____

August 10

Attend a staff development session to get some new ideas for your year.

_____

_____

_____

_____

August 11
Review the IEPs and evaluations for each of your students.

_____

_____

_____

_____

August 12
Outline a schedule for when student reevaluations are due and when IEPs are due.

_____

_____

_____

_____

August 13
Establish an e-mail user list for your parents so you can quickly send general messages about your class.

_____

_____

_____

_____

August 14
Purchase some thank-you notes, and set a goal to send at least five per week to faculty or parents who do something nice for you or your students.

_____

_____

_____

_____

August

August 15

If you don't have one, consider establishing a Web site for your class. If you have a Web site, prepare some sample home activities based on the needs of your students and the needs of the home.

_____

_____

_____

_____

August 16

Write a welcome note to the teachers and other staff who will be working with you.

_____

_____

_____

_____

August 17

Meet with the teachers who will be working with your students to discuss accommodations for your students and to determine their schedules.

_____

_____

_____

_____

August 18

After meeting with other teachers and related services personnel, set your schedule. Make sure your schedule depicts a high degree of engaged academic time for your students.

_____

_____

_____

_____

August 19

Prepare a resource list for the general education teachers in your building.

_____

_____

_____

_____

August 20

Go to lunch with some of your colleagues to share your summer activities.

_____

_____

_____

_____

August 21

Find out something unique and positive about your students. Prepare an opening-of-the-year story incorporating all the names of your students.

_____

_____

_____

_____

August 22

Prepare a homework tool kit for your parents.

_____

_____

_____

_____

August 23

Develop at least ten new ideas for alternatives to worksheets.

_____

_____

_____

_____

August 24

Develop at least three games for reinforcing specific skills.

_____

_____

_____

_____

August 25

Make bookmarks for your students with some key vocabulary words.

_____

_____

_____

_____

August 26

Search the Web for at least three new ideas to use in your classroom.

_____

_____

_____

_____

August 27

Go to the opening teachers' workshop with an attitude of enthusiasm and excitement. It is always fun to see everyone again.

_____

_____

_____

_____

August 28

Make the new teachers in your building feel welcome. Offer to help them or to share a book that you have found particularly helpful.

_____

_____

_____

_____

August 29

Make a resolution that you will make every effort to stay positive and not join in when colleagues become negative. Instead try to divert the discussion with positive statements.

_____

_____

_____

_____

August 30

Plan a series of icebreakers to use with students throughout the first week of school.

_____

_____

_____

_____

August 31

Reflect on how lucky you are to be working with your students and the faculty this year.

_____

_____

_____

_____

Additional Reflections

_____

_____

_____

_____

_____

_____

_____

_____

_____

_____

_____

_____

_____

_____

_____

_____

_____

_____

_____

_____

_____

_____

_____

_____

_____

_____

_____

Important Deadlines

_____

_____

_____

_____

_____

_____

_____

Things to Do in September

_____

_____

_____

_____

_____

_____

_____

_____

_____

_____

_____

_____

_____

_____

_____

_____

_____

_____

September

BUILDING TEAM RAPPORT WITH STAFF THROUGH CONSULTATION AND COLLABORATION

During September you may feel as if it is "uphill all the way," as there is so much to set up in terms of schedules and setting a positive tone with students. This is also a time to begin building positive relationships with staff. The tone set with other special educators and certainly all coworkers determines everyone's direction for the entire year.

Goals

_____

_____

_____

_____

_____

_____

_____

_____

_____

_____

September

September 1

Each staff person operates interdependently. As the school year begins, observe the many ways each person at your school impacts other adults whether positively or negatively.

_____

_____

_____

_____

September 2

Be aware of the multiple teams in which you participate both in your school and in your broader department.

_____

_____

_____

_____

September 3

At each IEP meeting, you create a team atmosphere for that particular time. See this gathering as an opportunity to also build community for the next time you meet.

_____

_____

_____

_____

September 4

As spontaneous teams of staff cluster to talk informally about a student's academic or behavioral issues, be certain the location of the discussion lends itself to confidentiality.

_____

_____

_____

_____

September 5

As part of a formal team meeting about a student, balance input and listening to contribute with insight and wisdom.

_____

_____

_____

_____

September 6

Determine times to meet with general education staff on a regular basis to stay on top of needs and concerns.

_____

_____

_____

_____

September 7

Keep the lines of communication open with all staff members, seeking from them ongoing informal observations relative to student learning and behavior.

_____

_____

_____

_____

September

September 8

Make a point of affirming how each person who interacts with your students benefits them. Affirmation of the school psychologist or the bus driver comes back to your students.

_____

_____

_____

_____

September 9

Find ways with general educators to mutually support one another's students. Be open to suggestions yourself, and offer others suggestions in a constructive manner.

_____

_____

_____

_____

September 10

Take time to get to know the personal side of the members of various teams in which you participate. Show interest in the topics beyond school that capture their attention.

_____

_____

_____

_____

September 11

Be alert to the growth areas of the teachers you support. Offer them books, articles, and information on workshops on relevant academic and behavioral topics.

_____

_____

_____

_____

September 12

Work with your administrators to open opportunities for teachers to attend professional conferences on topics to strengthen their expertise in using learning accommodations and adaptations for your students.

_____

_____

_____

_____

September 13

Survey staff members to learn where they want to develop strengths. Bring in speakers to help them grow in social and behavior training or in other areas of interest.

_____

_____

_____

_____

September 14

Find ways to use your budget to buy material that will bring general benefit to classrooms. Do they need technology, timers, or tactile materials that you could provide?

_____

_____

_____

_____

September

September 15

Find opportunities to get on the agenda for a staff meeting to share your expertise on a topic that will help your students better acclimate in mainstream classrooms.

_____

_____

_____

_____

September 16

Showing a DVD on bringing visual, auditory, kinesthetic, and tactile dimensions to lessons or on a specific disability area helps educate everyone. Bring snacks to facilitate team socialization.

_____

_____

_____

_____

September 17

When relating one on one with a team member, do what you expect of your students: Use good eye contact, listening skills, and a pleasant voice tone.

_____

_____

_____

_____

September 18

Reach out to team members when you need support or assistance. The memory of mutual support brings strength to teams and creates the momentum for further sharing.

_____

_____

_____

_____

September 19

Use folders and systems for written communication to stay in touch on a regular basis. Offer one another options beyond the formal meeting situations for sharing events and concerns.

_____

_____

_____

_____

September 20

Offer to teach demonstration lessons in general education classrooms to increase awareness of specific strategies that work best with your students and others in the group.

_____

_____

_____

_____

September 21

When in an intense meeting, mentally step back and observe the dynamics. Consider what you can do or say to help calm the waters or improve group focus.

_____

_____

_____

_____

September

September 22

Take every opportunity to be alert to ways that you can present big-picture thinking as well as precision understanding during a discussion about a particular student.

_____

_____

_____

_____

September 23

During a team meeting, speak strategically, and time your contributions for maximum impact on the group. Couple reason with emotions and use intuition and perception.

_____

_____

_____

_____

September 24

When meeting in a small or large group, be willing to reverse your opinion or bring out areas of controversy in a respectful manner to ultimately benefit students.

_____

_____

_____

_____

September 25

Be willing to credit team members for any contribution. When at a staff meeting, be sure to name the originators of constructive suggestions from your department.

_____

_____

_____

_____

September 26

Summarize what has occurred by linking successive contributions that have led to the current direction or final decision of the group.

_____

_____

_____

_____

September 27

Be a consistent personality with each member of the group whether you are meeting one on one or assembled as a team. This builds trust and respect.

_____

_____

_____

_____

September 28

Build alliances carefully with clear outcomes in mind. When there is conflict, be willing to take the time to reach a workable consensus.

_____

_____

_____

_____

September

September 29

When making an appointment with a teacher or an administrator, be sensitive to his or her time by coming prepared. Share concise and specific concerns, and work steadily for solutions.

_____

_____

_____

_____

September 30

Pause for laughter during team meetings or individual consultations. Take deep breaths and use emotions as cues to concerns as you bring them under the control of common sense.

_____

_____

_____

_____

Additional Reflections

_____

_____

_____

_____

_____

Additional Reflections

_____

_____

_____

_____

_____

_____

_____

_____

_____

_____

_____

_____

_____

_____

_____

_____

_____

_____

_____

_____

_____

_____

_____

_____

_____

_____

_____

Important Deadlines

_____

_____

_____

_____

_____

_____

_____

Things to Do in October

_____

_____

_____

_____

_____

_____

_____

_____

_____

_____

_____

_____

_____

_____

_____

_____

_____

_____

_____

Working Effectively With Parents

Parenting any child is a heavy responsibility. Parenting a child with special needs presents its own set of unique challenges. The parent of a child with disabilities has to fulfill the many roles of a parent as well as ensure that the additional medical and educational needs of the child are being met.

When we work with parents of children with special needs, we must always stop and think about those many challenges that the parents face and the impact those challenges have on the parents and the entire family. Parents may feel stressed and overwhelmed with all of their responsibilities. It is our job as special educators to provide support and positive feedback to them.

Goals

_____

_____

_____

_____

_____

_____

_____

 *October*

October 1

Learn as much as you can about the makeup/interests of the family before meeting with the family and working with the student. Learn about the other siblings in the home.

October 2

Avoid basing your opinion about the family on what colleagues may tell you.

October 3

Together with the social worker or another school staff member, make an appointment with the parents to visit within the home.

October 4

Parents may have negative feelings about schools and be reluctant to come for conferences. If so, arrange to meet with them at a neutral site, such as a local coffee shop.

_____

_____

_____

_____

October 5

When talking with a parent, always open with a smile and a positive statement.

_____

_____

_____

_____

October 6

Ask parents to evaluate any homework you give.

_____

_____

_____

_____

October 7

Set a goal for yourself to write at least two positive notes home to each parent per week.

_____

_____

_____

_____

 *October*

October 8

Instead of worksheets for homework, make a learning game for the child to take home to play.

_____

_____

_____

_____

October 9

When it is time for the Open House session, offer to take family pictures with your camera. This is a great incentive to get the parents to attend.

_____

_____

_____

_____

October 10

When you learn about new resources or parent trainings in your community, be sure to share those with the parent. Volunteer to attend a training session with the parent.

_____

_____

_____

_____

October 11

Ask parents for their birthdays, and send them birthday cards.

_____

_____

_____

_____

October 12

Plan for a holiday gift for your students and their families. Make a calendar with pictures of your class and ideas for parents.

_____

_____

_____

_____

October 13

Do a community service project that involves your families, such as a food drive or helping at a nursing home. This gives you a chance to talk with families as you help others together.

_____

_____

_____

_____

October 14

Work with the parents to establish a home-school communication system that will work best for them. It may be a daily notebook back and forth, an e-mail system, or a set phone call time. Capitalize on the parents' preferences.

_____

_____

_____

_____

 *October*

October 15

Prepare a test preparation kit for the family that includes materials needed for tests, a list of direction words, and stress-reduction activities.

_____

_____

_____

_____

October 16

Prepare a set of 3 × 5 cards of difficult vocabulary words, along with the definitions, and encourage the parents to play the game Concentration with their children to learn the words.

_____

_____

_____

_____

October 17

Make a list of individualized activities for the child based on the disability's impact on learning. If the child has difficulty with auditory memory, provide remediation and compensatory activities.

_____

_____

_____

_____

October 18

Talk with the parents about the importance of establishing their own set of special education records for their child. Provide them with suggestions on how to organize the records.

_____

_____

_____

_____

October 19

Stress to the parents that you want to work together as a team.

_____

_____

_____

_____

October 20

Establish a schedule for parents to come in to observe your work with their child. Make parents feel welcome within your classroom.

_____

_____

_____

_____

October 21

Download a game show from the Internet, and make a game that includes facts that you are studying with the student. Make a copy for the family to utilize with their child.

_____

_____

_____

_____

 *October*

October 22

Make a list of Web site resources for the family.

_____

_____

_____

_____

October 23

Each week send a helpful hint home for the parents.

_____

_____

_____

_____

October 24

Work with your principal to get funding for a small lending library for parents.

_____

_____

_____

_____

October 25

When a parent voices a concern, be sure to make a note about it, address it, and follow up to see if the parent feels the issue is resolved.

_____

_____

_____

_____

October 26

Before the student's IEP meeting, talk with the parents to determine whether they have any particular concerns that should be addressed at the time.

_____

_____

_____

_____

October 27

Before the IEP meeting, send the parents a draft of the information so they can review it ahead of time.

_____

_____

_____

_____

October 28

Encourage parents to avoid scary or violent activities at this time of year. Provide them with examples of nonviolent costume ideas, activities, or DVDs for Halloween.

_____

_____

_____

_____

October

October 29

   Provide parents with a list of alternative trick-or-treat gifts, such as Halloween pencils.

_____

_____

_____

_____

October 30

   Provide periodic nights at the movies for parents where you show a DVD about parenting a student with special needs or a DVD that explains about having a disability.

_____

_____

_____

_____

October 31

   Instead of having parents send in candy treats for Halloween, encourage them to join your class to watch a positive and happy video.

_____

_____

_____

_____

Additional Reflections

_____

_____

_____

_____

_____

_____

_____

_____

_____

_____

_____

_____

_____

_____

_____

_____

_____

_____

_____

_____

_____

_____

_____

_____

_____

_____

_____

_____

Important Deadlines

_____

_____

_____

_____

_____

_____

Things to Do in November

_____

_____

_____

_____

_____

_____

_____

_____

_____

_____

_____

_____

_____

_____

_____

_____

_____

_____

November

Writing and Applying Effective and Meaningful IEPs

The Individualized Education Program is the cornerstone of the child's special education program. It charts the course for the school year in the life of the child. It is the blueprint to ensure that the child gains meaningful benefit from an educational program. It is a comprehensive view of the child's background, strengths, and present levels of academic achievement and functional performance; parental concerns; and goals for the child and the specialized instruction and accommodations necessary to meet those goals.

As the special educator, you are charged with the serious responsibility of working with the child to ensure that he or she gains benefit over the course of the year. You monitor closely the child's progress and your work with the child. You also monitor to ensure that other service providers are following the IEP, and you lend your support to ensure that they also are meeting the child's needs.

Recognize that the IEP will impact the life of the child, and vow to ensure that the impact is positive.

Goals

_____

_____

_____

November

November 1

When writing IEPs and progress reports, avoid the use of educational jargon. Be as specific as possible about what you mean.

_____

_____

_____

_____

November 2

Review assessments and ensure that what are found as deficits are reflected in the goals for the student.

_____

_____

_____

_____

November 3

Make sure that strengths of the child are an integral part of the IEP and that those strengths are reflected in instruction.

_____

_____

_____

_____

November 4

Ensure that the goals of the student reflect the specific individualized needs of the student.

_____

_____

_____

_____

November 5

Establish a tickler system to monitor when IEPs are due for an annual review.

_____

_____

_____

_____

November 6

Even though your IEPs must be kept in a safe and locked place, be sure to keep them where you have ready access and can refer to them weekly.

_____

_____

_____

_____

November 7

Ensure that you write goals for students from an early age that set them up for success now and later in both academics and independent living.

_____

_____

_____

_____

November

November 8

The IEP must delineate both the specialized instruction needed for the student as well as necessary accommodations and modifications. Accommodations don't replace specialized instruction.

_____

_____

_____

_____

November 9

If behavior is impeding the learning of the student, discuss the need for a functional behavioral assessment and behavioral intervention plan with other members of the team.

_____

_____

_____

_____

November 10

When students participate in their own IEP meeting, prepare them by previewing what will be discussed.

_____

_____

_____

_____

November 11

Be sure to address parental concerns at the IEP meeting.

_____

_____

_____

_____

November 12

Prepare a fact sheet for parents and for general educators about the IEP process and what to expect; include an explanation of the importance of their role.

_____

_____

_____

_____

November 13

Work with the classroom teacher to ensure that he or she understands the specific needs of the student and the accommodations needed.

_____

_____

_____

_____

November 14

Provide IEP summary sheets for the classroom teachers. The summary sheet can provide an overview of the skills of the student, needs, and effective strategies.

_____

_____

_____

_____

November

November 15

Establish periodic informal reviews of the IEP with other members of the team.

_____

_____

_____

_____

November 16

Before the student's annual IEP meeting, meet with the parents to determine whether there are specific concerns that need to be addressed.

_____

_____

_____

_____

November 17

Time in IEP preparation is well spent. Prepare a draft and provide it to parents and other team members for their review before the meeting. Mark it as a "draft."

_____

_____

_____

_____

November 18

Keep a file folder of all forms that might be needed when you attend the IEP meeting. That way you are prepared and don't waste everyone's time going to get forms.

_____

_____

_____

_____

November 19

Before preparing a new IEP, review the previous one carefully, and note what the child has accomplished and what work is still needed.

_____

_____

_____

_____

November 20

Ensure there is enough specificity in the present levels of academic achievement and functional performance so that someone else has a clear picture of where the child is functioning.

_____

_____

_____

_____

November 21

At Thanksgiving time celebrate each child's progress. Show the child his progress toward his goals and recognize him for his achievements.

_____

_____

_____

_____

November

November 22

Celebrate your own accomplishments with the student as well.

_____

_____

_____

_____

November 23

Over Thanksgiving break ask yourself whether the IEPs are meeting the needs of the students. If not, vow to request a new IEP meeting when you return from vacation.

_____

_____

_____

_____

November 24

Reflect on your own behavior after every IEP meeting. Did you actively engage the parents in the process? Did you encourage others to speak? Were you organized?

_____

_____

_____

_____

November 25

Monitor your own behavior to determine whether you are devoting the time outlined on the IEP to specific instruction or giving students busywork to get paperwork done.

_____

_____

_____

_____

November 26

Talk with the parents after the IEP meeting to get their feedback on the process and to determine whether they are satisfied with the outcome.

_____

_____

_____

_____

November 27

Collect data to determine whether the student is making progress toward his or her goals.

_____

_____

_____

_____

November 28

Make an outline of what you want to cover at the IEP meeting. Stick to the point. If you do get off track, reflect after the meeting on what you could do differently.

_____

_____

_____

_____

November 29

This is a good time to reflect on whether you are following the IEPs and how well the student is doing.

_____

_____

_____

_____

November 30

Take PRIDE in the IEP.

    P   Preparation.
    R   Review the previous IEP.
    I   Individualized.
    D   Data based.
    E   Every IEP participant provides input.

Before the IEP meeting, review the latest evaluation and incorporate that information into the document and the discussion.

Monitor that the amount of special education and related services that are in the IEP are actually the time that is being provided.

_____

_____

_____

_____

Additional Reflections

_____

_____

_____

_____

_____

_____

_____

_____

_____

_____

_____

_____

_____

_____

_____

_____

_____

_____

_____

_____

_____

_____

_____

_____

_____

Important Deadlines

_____

_____

_____

_____

_____

_____

_____

Things to Do in December

_____

_____

_____

_____

_____

_____

_____

_____

_____

_____

_____

_____

_____

_____

_____

_____

_____

KEEPING FOCUSED AND ORGANIZED

During December we are all on circuit overload. We have not only all of our usual responsibilities but also the holiday festivities, special programs, gifts to purchase, and more. We find ourselves overcommitting and getting stressed out. If you live in some parts of the country, you hope for a "snow day" so you can get caught up. Added to the stress of getting everything done is the likelihood that your students are all wound up with all of the holiday hubbub, and it is hard to keep them focused. This is the time of year when we all need to keep focused and organized so that we can enjoy the holidays without worrying about getting everything done. This month provides you with some helpful hints. Happy Holidays to you!

Goals

_____

_____

_____

_____

_____

_____

_____

December

December 1

When faced with a large task, break it down into small steps, and set deadlines for each of those steps.

_____

_____

_____

_____

December 2

Develop a calendar and reminder system that works for you—whether it be a daily, weekly, monthly, or electronic system.

_____

_____

_____

_____

December 3

Avoid overextending yourself. Don't volunteer for more projects because you know this month will be busy.

_____

_____

_____

_____

December 4

Try to get as much of the paperwork done from one day on that same day so you can start each day with a clean slate.

_____

_____

_____

_____

December 5

Establish a budget for what you will spend this month, and stay within that budget. Overspending causes more stress.

_____

_____

_____

_____

December 6

When getting frustrated with a task, walk away for five or ten minutes. Then return.

_____

_____

_____

_____

December 7

When you find yourself procrastinating from completing a major project, tell yourself you will start the task and work on it for five or ten minutes. You will find yourself working longer.

_____

_____

_____

_____

December

December 8

Spend a few minutes at the day's end having your students put things away within the classroom. This is teaching children a life skill and is a help to you.

_____

_____

_____

_____

December 9

Write up parent conferences or incident logs as soon as possible after the event; otherwise you forget important facts.

_____

_____

_____

_____

December 10

Keep the items you use most frequently close to you.

_____

_____

_____

_____

December 11

Establish a place for everything, and create your organizational system around those places.

_____

_____

_____

_____

December 12

Make lists in this calendar on what you determine to be your priorities for the day.

_____

_____

_____

_____

December 13

Use Post-it notes to help you remember to get something done. When the task is done, you can throw the Post-it note away.

_____

_____

_____

_____

December 14

A good friend used to set the table for breakfast the night before. Lesson learned: Get things ready for the next day the night before.

_____

_____

_____

_____

December

December 15

If you don't need a hard copy of the report sent to you electronically, save the file in the computer and don't print it.

_____

_____

_____

_____

December 16

This is a good month to look for shortcuts; for example, pay an organization to wrap your gifts or engage in a cookie exchange to reduce the number of cookies you have to bake.

_____

_____

_____

_____

December 17

Spend your time in proactive and positive activities rather than expending energy on negativity and complaining.

_____

_____

_____

_____

December 18

Establish your priorities for the day and week, and make sure you spend the majority of your time on those priorities.

_____

_____

_____

_____

December 19

Focus on your priorities first so you can get the priorities completed early.

_____

_____

_____

_____

December 20

When you are feeling worn out and overwhelmed, participate in some professional development activity to rejuvenate.

_____

_____

_____

_____

December 21

Learn the time of day you work best, and do your most difficult projects at that time.

_____

_____

_____

_____

December

December 22

Try getting up fifteen minutes earlier than usual to get a head start on the day.

_____

_____

_____

_____

December 23

Assess frequently the work you are doing with students to ensure that what you are doing is making a positive difference in their instruction and behavior.

_____

_____

_____

_____

December 24

Begin a new family tradition that requires a team effort and doesn't put all the work on you, for example, popping corn and watching a movie or looking at old family pictures.

_____

_____

_____

_____

December 25

Pause to reflect on the many treasures of life that you have: your family, home, friends.

_____

_____

_____

_____

December 26

Set a project goal, and when you reach the goal, reward yourself.

_____

_____

_____

_____

December 27

Catch up on some of your e-mails or paperwork today. Delete old e-mails and throw away old papers.

_____

_____

_____

_____

December 28

This is a good sale time. Buy yourself some organizational tools to prepare for the new year.

_____

_____

_____

_____

December

December 29

Buy a supply of greeting cards and other note cards, and keep them on hand to use when you need one.

_____

_____

_____

_____

December 30

Spend some time thinking about your time-wasters, and come up with a plan to reduce those in the new year.

_____

_____

_____

_____

December 31

Spend time today reflecting on your many accomplishments of the year, and pat yourself on the back for all you have done.

_____

_____

_____

_____

Additional Reflections

_____

_____

_____

_____

_____

_____

_____

_____

_____

_____

_____

_____

_____

_____

_____

_____

_____

_____

_____

_____

_____

_____

_____

_____

_____

_____

Important Deadlines

_____

_____

_____

_____

_____

_____

_____

Things to Do in January

_____

_____

_____

_____

_____

_____

_____

_____

_____

_____

_____

_____

_____

_____

_____

_____

_____

_____

Utilizing the Principles of Specialized Instruction

What is special about special education? It should be the intensive specialized instruction that is provided to the student that is based on that student's individualized needs. It is not one-size-fits-all instruction where every student gets the same thing rather than instruction based on what the student needs. Even though we must provide our students with disabilities the accommodations and modifications they need, we must also teach them the skills according to the most effective instructional methods. It is not enough to accommodate a student who can't read by reading to the student or utilizing books on tape; we must also teach the child to read. This month we focus on the critical components of specialized instruction. As our New Year's resolution, we need to continually reflect on the methods that we are utilizing with each student with whom we work, assuring that we are providing intensive, specialized instruction.

Goals

_____

_____

_____

_____

January

January 1

As a New Year's resolution, vow to continuously reflect on the methods you are utilizing with your students to determine whether your methods are based on your students' individualized needs.

_____

_____

_____

_____

January 2

Resolve to provide as much intensive individualized instruction to each student as you can.

_____

_____

_____

_____

January 3

Vow to reduce the amount of busy work that you may give students, and replace it with individualized instruction.

_____

_____

_____

_____

January 4

Before utilizing any instructional intervention, learn as much as possible about it to ensure that you are able to implement the intervention with integrity.

_____

_____

_____

_____

January 5

Before giving a student any worksheet or homework, ask yourself whether you have provided the necessary instruction for the student to do that assignment.

_____

_____

_____

_____

January 6

Frequently review the goals on each student's IEP, and ask yourself whether you are providing the necessary instruction to meet those goals.

_____

_____

_____

_____

January 7

Think about the amount of meaningful engaged time you give your students. What can you do to maximize that engaged time?

_____

_____

_____

_____

January 8

Identify the barriers that prevent you from providing intensive, specialized instruction, and work with your supervisor to see what can be done to increase the individualized time you can spend with the student.

_____

_____

_____

_____

January 9

Review the most recent comprehensive evaluations on each of your students. Look for patterns of how the student learns.

_____

_____

_____

_____

January 10

Specialized instruction should focus on both remediation and compensation.

_____

_____

_____

_____

January 11

The purpose of remediation is to improve specific skill deficits.

_____

_____

_____

_____

January 12

The purpose of compensation is to teach the child to use his or her strengths to learn best.

_____

_____

_____

_____

January 13

Ensure that the instructional methods you are using are research-based interventions.

_____

_____

_____

_____

January 14

Through systematic observations, learn as much as possible about how the child learns best.

_____

_____

_____

_____

January

January 15

Interview the parents to get an idea of how they believe their child learns best.

_____

_____

_____

_____

January 16

Talk to previous teachers of the student, and take notes on what they say worked with the student and what didn't work.

_____

_____

_____

_____

January 17

Utilize the diagnostic prescriptive approach where you test, teach, test, reteach. Remember that testing can be formal or informal but always is used to improve instruction.

_____

_____

_____

_____

January 18

If the student has a learning disability, identify the processing deficit: auditory memory, written language, or visual perceptual skills.

_____

_____

_____

_____

January 19

If the student has memory deficits, what mnemonic strategies are you teaching to assist the student?

_____

_____

_____

_____

January 20

Teach your students as much as possible about their specific disability.

_____

_____

_____

_____

January 21

Teach self-management strategies so students can chart their own progress.

_____

_____

_____

_____

January

January 22

Involve students in graphing their own progress on specific target areas, such as reading recognition or math facts.

_____

_____

_____

_____

January 23

Collect data continuously on whether your reading, math, or writing instruction is resulting in improvement in the student's skills. Progress monitoring is critical.

_____

_____

_____

_____

January 24

If the student is not making progress with the specific instructional strategies you are using, investigate why and determine whether a new IEP meeting should be called.

_____

_____

_____

_____

January 25

Learn the strengths of each of your students so you can incorporate them into the specialized instruction.

_____

_____

_____

_____

January 26

Utilize multisensory techniques that include visual, auditory, tactile, and kinesthetic modes of instruction.

_____

_____

_____

_____

January 27

Learn as much as possible about the cultural needs of the student, and incorporate those needs into your instruction.

_____

_____

_____

_____

January 28

Determine the specific triggers for student behaviors, and teach your students to identify those triggers.

_____

_____

_____

_____

January

January 29

Learn as much as possible about the sensory needs of the student and build those into instruction. Does the student need movement? Do bright lights bother him or her?

_____

_____

_____

_____

January 30

Expose students to a variety of ways to organize assignments and materials so they can learn what ways work best for them.

_____

_____

_____

_____

January 31

Because learning is emotional, discover as much as you can about the child's emotional barriers or anxieties about certain subjects.

_____

_____

_____

_____

Additional Reflections

_____

_____

_____

_____

_____

_____

_____

_____

_____

_____

_____

_____

_____

_____

_____

_____

_____

_____

_____

_____

_____

_____

_____

_____

_____

_____

_____

_____

_____

_____

Important Deadlines

_____

_____

_____

_____

_____

_____

Things to Do in February

_____

_____

_____

_____

_____

_____

_____

_____

_____

_____

_____

_____

_____

_____

MAINTAINING YOUR IDEALS THROUGH REFLECTION AND ACTION

Everyone has times of certainty about personal beliefs and identity. Yet, because of unforeseen external circumstances, great or small, it's easy to lose that sense of bedrock certainty in exchange for confusion, waffling on assurances, and feelings of being turned upside down.

Special educators who regain this assurance step back and reflect, gain their confidence, and determine a plan of action as a result. By taking this time for reflection, action in school better coordinates with personal belief and identity.

Goals

_____

_____

_____

_____

_____

_____

_____

_____

February

February 1

Take ten minutes to list ten beliefs that you hold regarding special education.

_____

_____

_____

_____

February 2

Quickly list ten positive adjectives to describe yourself as a special educator.

_____

_____

_____

_____

February 3

Determine a personalized action plan regarding how to best deal with challenging student behavior in an emergency. Keep it in your plan book for immediate access.

_____

_____

_____

_____

February 4

Describe in writing who you are at your most competent level when speaking with a parent.

_____

_____

_____

_____

February 5

If a general educator were to tell another teacher how you relate optimally with your peers, what would that person say? Keep your description in a safe but accessible spot.

_____

_____

_____

_____

February 6

Realize that any of the descriptions that you have written are vulnerable to personalities, events, and the unexpected changes of school life.

_____

_____

_____

_____

February 7

Find time today to reflect on small occurrences that have caused you to lose your game plan. Take note of what happens to your feelings, mood, and reaction.

_____

_____

_____

_____

February

February 8

Write on a small index card the one characteristic that helps you bounce back the quickest from being thrown off your game. Keep it in your wallet or planner.

_____

_____

_____

_____

February 9

When you notice an event that throws you off course today, take a deep breath, recall the word on your card, and review it if you have the time.

_____

_____

_____

_____

February 10

Imagine yourself free today to go to a quiet place of your choosing to gain perspective on a key school challenge. What would be your new view of the situation?

_____

_____

_____

_____

February 11

Be alert for the rise of any anger today, and save your memories of it for later. Take time after school to journal about what you felt and why.

_____

_____

_____

_____

February 12

Today be on the lookout for feelings of fear in terms of your relationships or your sense of competence. List what has set off those fears.

_____

_____

_____

_____

February 13

Notice things about your job that you cannot change at all. What kind of attitude will you take toward these people or events?

_____

_____

_____

_____

February 14

What do you love the most about your current teaching situation? How do you express your educational ideals around that?

_____

_____

_____

_____

February

February 15

Recall what you consider the greatest catastrophe you have experienced so far this year. How did you handle it? What might you do differently the next time something "big" happens?

_____

_____

_____

_____

February 16

Review a book or an article about special education to help gain grounding and focus today.

_____

_____

_____

_____

February 17

Observe another special education professional as to how he or she holds on to idealism, balance, and emotional evenness.

_____

_____

_____

_____

February 18

When things become more intense today, focus on an object in the room for the count of five. Then resume your activity aiming for more clarity and purpose.

_____

_____

_____

_____

February 19

Place an item in your pocket—such as a rock, meaningful medallion, textured cloth, or photo—that helps you come back to balance and certainty as needed.

_____

_____

_____

_____

February 20

Determine a spot in the building to go to regroup. Place a tiny object there that only you know about. Let it cue you for perspective regarding your worthy endeavors.

_____

_____

_____

_____

February 21

Send yourself an e-mail to a nonschool account, or call your home answering machine with a word of encouragement that you would like to hear from another.

_____

_____

_____

_____

February

February 22

Review your beliefs from February 1, and visualize yourself applying them to your situation today.

_____

_____

_____

_____

February 23

Note on your calendar a time within the next two weeks when you will get away for one to three hours of personal reflection time.

_____

_____

_____

_____

February 24

Recall someone in the field who has inspired you in the past. Imagine that person alongside you today offering encouragement.

_____

_____

_____

_____

February 25

Imagine one student five years from now who will be better because of something you did today.

_____

_____

_____

_____

February 26

Find an inspirational quote to keep on your desk that helps reroute your thoughts toward your purpose for being a special education teacher.

_____

_____

_____

_____

February 27

When something unexpected happens today that could potentially discourage you, use it as a signal to be grateful for being in special education.

_____

_____

_____

_____

February 28

When passing in the hall today, stop to speak to a student you wouldn't normally talk to. Consider this contact as a moment for reflection on the value of every student.

_____

_____

_____

_____

February

February 29

Take a leap of faith today and visualize yourself acting from your highest ideal as a special educator during a typical exchange with a parent, a colleague, a student, or an administrator.

_____

_____

_____

_____

Additional Reflections

_____

_____

_____

_____

_____

_____

_____

_____

_____

_____

_____

_____

_____

Additional Reflections

_____

_____

_____

_____

_____

_____

_____

_____

_____

_____

_____

_____

_____

_____

_____

_____

_____

_____

_____

_____

_____

_____

_____

_____

_____

_____

_____

_____

_____

Important Deadlines

_____

_____

_____

_____

_____

_____

_____

Things to Do in March

_____

_____

_____

_____

_____

_____

_____

_____

_____

_____

_____

_____

_____

_____

_____

_____

_____

_____

FINDING THE SUPPORT AND STRENGTH YOU NEED TO DO YOUR JOB

Working in the field of special education presents many challenges. Though special educators must be strong individuals to stand up for students and families and to meet the unexpected at every turn, one cannot go the distance alone. Given the complex nature of special education, support from others is essential to maintain balance and perspective.

Goals

_____

_____

_____

_____

_____

_____

_____

_____

_____

_____

March

March 1

Identify those individuals in your buildings who are good listeners and can keep information confidential. Seek them out when you need support and assistance.

_____

_____

_____

_____

March 2

Determine to establish a steady partnership with one or a few colleagues in your school who can offer helpful feedback on how you relate with a challenging student.

_____

_____

_____

_____

March 3

Contact a teacher in another building whose job is similar to yours. Keep in touch with this person who can understand your situation well.

_____

_____

_____

_____

March 4

Be willing to contact your supervisors when you need their advice and assistance with the system or with a family.

_____

_____

_____

_____

March 5

Attend professional networking events. Listen carefully to what others say for similarities to your concerns and personal validation. Stay in touch with those who understand your perspective.

_____

_____

_____

_____

March 6

Consider who in your broader world offers you affirmation and encouragement. Seek such persons out with a phone call, an e-mail, a text message, or a note.

_____

_____

_____

_____

March 7

Get together for a walk or coffee with someone outside of education to exchange general thoughts and specific ideas about work.

_____

_____

_____

_____

March

March 8

List names of professionals, clergy, or support groups to save for times when things at school remain overwhelming for a long stretch.

_____

_____

_____

_____

March 9

Be open to the wisdom of school staff in other roles. Those who work for food service or who do clerical or cleaning work have a valuable view of school situations.

_____

_____

_____

_____

March 10

Get involved with professional groups that exist to advance the cause of special education. Live their mission and implement their vision. Take courage and energy from their collective dream.

_____

_____

_____

_____

March 11

Take time to write in your journal so you can go to your core in search of your fortitude and determination. Reenter your school setting in touch with your inner substance.

_____

_____

_____

_____

March 12

Know your limits on any given day. Have a back-up plan to replenish your energy in the evening.

_____

_____

_____

_____

March 13

Keep affirmations at hand that reinforce your talent as a special educator. Review them systematically.

_____

_____

_____

_____

March 14

Avoid negative staff members who denigrate the value of special education. In contrast, work to build rapport with general and special educators who have a heart for your students and appreciate your work.

_____

_____

_____

_____

March 15

Offer your time to listen to a beginning special education teacher. This not only builds a relationship but also reinforces what you have to offer the field.

_____

_____

_____

_____

March 16

Save notes, e-mails, and words of praise when you get them from students, families, and colleagues. When your well runs dry, read these out loud to yourself.

_____

_____

_____

_____

March 17

Look for an exchange with a staff member today that could not be possible if you were not a special educator. Be grateful for that moment.

_____

_____

_____

_____

March 18

Watch one of your students perform a task that could not have been done unless you had taught the skill that enabled this young person to proceed to this next step.

_____

_____

_____

_____

March 19

Search out a paper you did when you were studying to enter this field. Own the learning you received from the exercise.

_____

_____

_____

_____

March 20

Look for a training session or workshop that would give you more confidence in social skills or a curricular area where you need growth.

_____

_____

_____

_____

March 21

Pick the brain of another special educator in regard to how this person deals with challenging student behavior.

_____

_____

_____

_____

March 22

Randomly ask a general educator about key strategies to support a student who is struggling. Use this exchange to build a bridge and enhance your own teaching.

_____

_____

_____

_____

March 23

Keep tabs on ways you have grown. Consider the strengths you have developed since you have begun working in special education.

_____

_____

_____

_____

March 24

Sort out in your mind the staff members who are really with you and who trust you. Resolve to thank them soon for their support.

_____

_____

_____

_____

March 25

Give up any self-doubt about your value to the field of special education. Know that your commitment and presence has a long-term effect on those around you.

_____

_____

_____

_____

March 26

Renew your relationship with a classmate from teacher training. Share the status of your ideals and expectations in comparison to when you were in school together.

_____

_____

_____

_____

March 27

Invite a child study team member or general educator to stop in after school for a treat. Take time to laugh at a student comment or express any frustrations about the day.

_____

_____

_____

_____

March 28

Use your creativity and initiative to set up a group to talk about a topic of interest in special education.

_____

_____

_____

_____

March

March 29

This evening, as you reflect back on the school day, review the many exchanges you have had that increased your sense of purpose and professionalism.

_____

_____

_____

_____

March 30

Seek out support from an unlikely source today. This could be the passing smile of a clerk at the drugstore or the matter-of-fact acceptance of your work from a staff person or parent.

_____

_____

_____

_____

March 31

Cultivate a relationship with a retired special educator. This teacher can offer you a wealth of wisdom and invaluable support from years of experience in the field.

_____

_____

_____

_____

Additional Reflections

_____
_____
_____
_____
_____
_____
_____
_____
_____
_____
_____
_____
_____
_____
_____
_____
_____
_____
_____
_____
_____
_____
_____
_____
_____
_____

Important Deadlines

_____

_____

_____

_____

_____

_____

_____

Things to Do in April

_____

_____

_____

_____

_____

_____

_____

_____

_____

_____

_____

_____

_____

_____

_____

_____

_____

WORKING WITH ADMINISTRATORS AND THE GREATER COMMUNITY

We live in a social world that requires us to work collaboratively with many individuals: parents, administrators, and people in the larger community within which we live. We cannot remain behind the closed doors of our classroom but must interact continually with many individuals.

Our ability to work together with individuals will determine our success within the special education field. With our students with special needs, we focus on teaching them appropriate social skills, communicating and getting along with people around them. We must also focus our own career on those skills that will be a major contributor to our success. This month's ideas provide helpful hints for your positive involvement with administrators and with the greater community.

Goals

_____

_____

_____

_____

_____

April

April 1

Keep your building administrator and supervisor informed of what you are doing and issues being faced.

_____

_____

_____

_____

April 2

Document in writing all contacts with parents and other agencies, and provide a copy to your administrator.

_____

_____

_____

_____

April 3

Be an active and positive member of faculty meetings. Approach a problem with the attitude "what can we do together to improve the situation?"

_____

_____

_____

_____

April 4

When presented with a new idea from the administrator that you are skeptical about, ask questions to gain more information about the idea.

_____

_____

_____

_____

April 5

Always live up to your commitments. When you volunteer to serve on a committee, you have a responsibility to carry out the necessary tasks.

_____

_____

_____

_____

April 6

Avoid negative conversations about the administrator in the teachers' lounge or other locations.

_____

_____

_____

_____

April 7

Engage in active listening when talking to the administrator rather than interrupting with your own ideas.

_____

_____

_____

_____

April

April 8

When faced with a problem with a student or a parent, ask the administrator for his or her advice.

_____

_____

_____

_____

April 9

Recognize the constraints under which the administrator may be working. Try to see an issue from his or her point of view.

_____

_____

_____

_____

April 10

Whenever the administrator engages in a supportive act, remember to thank him or her. Jot a thank-you note or send an e-mail.

_____

_____

_____

_____

April 11

Learn the behaviors that please the administrator and work to engage in those behaviors, for example, arriving promptly for faculty meetings.

_____

_____

_____

_____

April 12

Learn the administrator's pet peeves, and avoid those behaviors.

_____

_____

_____

_____

April 13

Respond to the administrator's requests as soon as possible; reply to e-mails quickly.

_____

_____

_____

_____

April 14

When the administrator asks for input on an issue, provide constructive comments.

_____

_____

_____

_____

April

April 15

Ask the administrator to be a reinforcer for your students rather than a punisher.

_____

_____

_____

_____

April 16

When faced with a problem with the administrator, talk to the administrator first and try to work it out proactively.

_____

_____

_____

_____

April 17

When your administrator is worthy, nominate him or her for an award for contributions made.

_____

_____

_____

_____

April 18

Invite your administrator to your classroom for special activities.

_____

_____

_____

_____

April 19

Praise your administrator publicly when he or she supports you.

_____

_____

_____

_____

April 20

Designate a Principal's Appreciation Week within your classroom, and each day have your students do something positive for the administrator.

_____

_____

_____

_____

April 21

At the end of the day, share something positive that happened in your classroom. Administrators often hear only the negative; they relish positive happenings.

_____

_____

_____

_____

April

April 22

Remember that you are a positive ambassador for special education in the community and should speak positively about your work.

_____

_____

_____

_____

April 23

Get involved in community organizations to get to know individuals in other fields. Their perspective is helpful to know.

_____

_____

_____

_____

April 24

With clearance from your building administrator, offer to speak to community organizations about special education.

_____

_____

_____

_____

April 25

Involve your students in community service projects so the community sees the positive contributions your students can make.

_____

_____

_____

_____

April 26

For Exceptional Children's Week, offer to write an article for the newspaper about the accomplishments of students with special needs.

_____

_____

_____

_____

April 27

Invite community members to come to your class to speak about their careers.

_____

_____

_____

_____

April 28

Recognize community members who contribute to special education programs in your area.

_____

_____

_____

_____

April

April 29

Work with your administrator to do a joint presentation to the school board about what is happening in your classroom.

_____

_____

_____

_____

April 30

Volunteer to serve on community task forces.

_____

_____

_____

_____

Additional Reflections

_____

_____

_____

_____

_____

_____

_____

Additional Reflections

Important Deadlines

_____

_____

_____

_____

_____

_____

_____

Things to Do in May

_____

_____

_____

_____

_____

_____

_____

_____

_____

_____

_____

_____

_____

_____

_____

_____

_____

MANAGING THE STRESS
OF CLOSING OUT THE SCHOOL YEAR

The last days of the school year prove a sharp contrast to the new life of spring presented by nature. For many in northern climates, the return of warmth and sunshine invites outside activity, relaxation, and openness to change. For those in warmer areas, spring still speaks of joy and new life.

However, events inside any school building occur in stark contrast to that. Incredible demands, deadlines, and difficulties underlie the duties typical of any school day. Special educators must conclude IEPs by certain dates, keep their students afloat, wrap up reports, and close the room while maintaining rapport with staff and families. This is no easy task. However, if managed with deliberateness and patience, special educators can do it.

Goals

_____

_____

_____

_____

_____

May 1

In spite of the job demands, acknowledge the beauty of the season by walking outside and delighting in nature.

_____

_____

_____

_____

May 2

Resolve to enjoy the season's gifts. Plan outdoor outings for each weekend to keep you going during the upcoming intensity.

_____

_____

_____

_____

May 3

Pull out and prioritize IEP meeting dates. Work systematically at all details relative to each upcoming meeting.

_____

_____

_____

_____

May 4

Find an ally who aims for equanimity. Check in from time to time for perspective.

_____

_____

_____

_____

May 5

Know that when staff members feel pressure, they are not themselves. Be forgiving of short tempers and curt comments.

_____

_____

_____

_____

May 6

Always remember how close you are to summer in spite of how insurmountable the paperwork seems.

_____

_____

_____

_____

May 7

Utilize the assistance of paraprofessionals and volunteers to free yourself for doing what only you can do.

_____

_____

_____

_____

May

May 8

Keep your head above water through humor. Whose sense of humor can help filter your perceptions?

_____

_____

_____

_____

May 9

Limit the amount of work you take home to allow for social or down time.

_____

_____

_____

_____

May 10

Stay in touch with someone outside special education to remain in the flow of life outside your office or center.

_____

_____

_____

_____

May 11

Check in with another special education teacher by e-mail. Give mutual encouragement and understanding.

_____

_____

_____

_____

May 12

Realize that this peak of intensity at work will be followed by the complete opposite. Prepare yourself for the contrast.

_____

_____

_____

_____

May 13

Contact your special education secretary to gain some insight into how everyone is coping with the year-end frenzy. She may have some humorous stories to share.

_____

_____

_____

_____

May 14

Connect to birdsongs that reach you from outside. Can you name these songsters?

_____

_____

_____

_____

May

May 15

While being faithful to a "to-do" list, take time for deep breaths throughout the day.

_____

_____

_____

_____

May 16

Check with all your administrators to ensure that there are no surprises in terms of what you need to complete.

_____

_____

_____

_____

May 17

Check with special educators in your buildings about helping one another meet site expectations, especially if you serve multiple settings.

_____

_____

_____

_____

May 18

Negotiate as a team about who will attend various meetings and represent special education at IEP meetings and building events.

_____

_____

_____

_____

May 19

Plan a stay-late-at-work night with a colleague. After a determined time, go out for a walk or a late dinner to relax.

_____

_____

_____

_____

May 20

Credit yourself to a coworker for completing any task bringing you closer to the end of year deadline: "Done."

_____

_____

_____

_____

May 21

Enlist the help of family members on home duties, offering to make the favors up to them during the summer.

_____

_____

_____

_____

May

May 22

Bring something delightfully delicious as a lounge treat to recognize the efforts of the staff to complete everything on time.

_____

_____

_____

_____

May 23

Balance an occasional food indulgence with healthful eating to maintain momentum and energy.

_____

_____

_____

_____

May 24

Are you staying the course with stretching, weight training, and aerobic exercise?

_____

_____

_____

_____

May 25

Create goodwill by having your students draw pictures or write notes commending the staff for contributing to their education.

_____

_____

_____

_____

May 26

Inject positive comments into the school atmosphere by mentioning efforts of general education teachers and other staff members.

_____

_____

_____

_____

May 27

Monitor your anger and frustration so that your feelings do not come out sideways.

_____

_____

_____

_____

May 28

Multitask when possible, and focus on one thing with intensity when accuracy demands it.

_____

_____

_____

_____

May

May 29

Learn from your students to simplify life and anticipate the summer ahead.

_____

_____

_____

_____

May 30

Stop at a beautiful spot on the way home to acknowledge the seasonal delights you have sacrificed for your job.

_____

_____

_____

_____

May 31

To remain focused on priorities, list tasks you could complete by coming in after school has ended, just in case.

_____

_____

_____

_____

Additional Reflections

_____

_____

_____

_____

_____

_____

_____

_____

_____

_____

_____

_____

_____

_____

_____

_____

_____

_____

_____

_____

_____

_____

_____

_____

Important Deadlines

_____

_____

_____

_____

_____

_____

_____

Things to Do in June

_____

_____

_____

_____

_____

_____

_____

_____

_____

_____

_____

_____

_____

_____

_____

_____

_____

_____

LOOKING AT THE BIG PICTURE

Viewing Your Career Long-Term

Often tied up with the details of special education, teachers become focused on the moment, on the day, on their present circumstances. Going forward full throttle with the demands of the job, it is all that a person can do to manage the situations that occur each day and plan for handling what is expected tomorrow.

Then comes the unexpected—and a special educator must then regroup and address the unforeseen circumstances that rear up every day. Now with summer vacation coming, the routine of the regular school year will be over, presenting the opportunity to envision your career long term.

Goals

_____

_____

_____

_____

_____

_____

June

June 1

Now just be aware of the importance of being in the moment as you work with your students, parents, and staff.

_____

_____

_____

_____

June 2

Full attention to present detail will bring you capably to the end of this school year.

_____

_____

_____

_____

June 3

When thoughts of what you will do this summer come to mind, jot them down, and return to the present moment to efficiently complete the demands of the day.

_____

_____

_____

_____

June 4

Buy a notebook and title it "My Career Future." Carry it in your briefcase or backpack to collect spontaneous thoughts, or save it for summer reflection time ahead.

_____

_____

_____

_____

June 5

Now that you have given yourself permission to dream, be especially aware of any new career-related thoughts that surface. Put them in your notebook at the first possible time.

_____

_____

_____

_____

June 5

Casually observe those who work in other roles in your school. Consider aspects of their jobs that you might enjoy. Note those.

_____

_____

_____

_____

June 6

Invite your special education peers to share their plans for summer education and the reasons for their selections.

_____

_____

_____

_____

June

June 7

Consider a summer workshop to stretch your current skills and expertise. Consider how this would impact your future professional work.

_____
_____
_____
_____

June 8

Observe senior colleagues, and determine if what they are doing and how they work as professionals is a fit for your future.

_____
_____
_____
_____

June 9

When you drive home, let your mind wander to a typical day four years in the future. What thoughts will you have on the drive home then?

_____
_____
_____
_____

June 10

If a fictitious life coach asked you to rate your current job satisfaction on a scale from 1 to 10, 10 being the highest, how would you rate your present job?

_____

_____

_____

_____

June 11

Fold a page in your notebook in half. Head the first column "10 Preferred" and the second column "10 Less Preferred." Sort the features of your job accordingly.

_____

_____

_____

_____

June 12

Put these twenty features of your job on note cards, and rank them according to what you most prefer to be doing. Let that sit for twenty-four hours.

_____

_____

_____

_____

June 13

Review your list from yesterday and make any changes in the order of the cards.

_____

_____

_____

_____

June

June 14

Imagine a role in education that more exclusively includes your top three cards.

_____

_____

_____

_____

June 15

Look at your bottom three items and imagine creative ways to include these in an educational dream job of your choice.

_____

_____

_____

_____

June 16

If you had the option of starting in a new education job next fall, would you? How would that role compare to what you are now doing?

_____

_____

_____

_____

June 17

Do you prefer special education work in the same setting each day or do you like itinerant work better? Do you prefer more child-focused work or working with adults?

_____

_____

_____

_____

June 18

As you continue in your notebook, list three ways you could most grow in your field.

_____

_____

_____

_____

June 19

Ask a friend in another job how he or she would suggest that you could grow in the skills you have listed.

_____

_____

_____

_____

June 20

Go to a fresh page of your notebook. In big bold letters, list one career-related thing that you would love to do but for some reason think you could never do.

_____

_____

_____

_____

June 21

Whether what you wrote yesterday was to speak at a national conference, lead a parent group, or start your own tutoring business, own that you have had the thought or desire.

_____

_____

_____

_____

June 22

Note how your special education talents best serve others. Would there be a way to repackage them in another arena?

_____

_____

_____

_____

June 23

Be aware of any overt or subtle ways that your peers keep you from achieving a more fulfilling special education career. Keep an ongoing record of these observations.

_____

_____

_____

_____

June 24

When you walk into school each day, what are the first tasks that you typically go to? Do these selections have any bearing on ways to develop your career?

_____

_____

_____

_____

June 25

Search the Internet for special education jobs as if you were beginning again. What draws you? Do you find options for a new job or inclusion in your current job?

_____

_____

_____

_____

June 26

If you were going to speak to preservice teachers about going into special education, what would you name as the great gifts and opportunities of this educational role?

_____

_____

_____

_____

June 27

Notice your emotional life when you are away from special education. What do you miss doing now on a daily basis?

_____

_____

_____

_____

June 28

Project yourself ahead and see yourself as a retired special education teacher. If you could ask this future you about "wish I hads," what would you tell yourself?

_____

_____

_____

_____

June 29

Journal about what you need in your professional life that you would miss on a deep level if life circumstances changed overnight and you had to leave your job.

_____

_____

_____

_____

June 30

Get in touch with your personal sense of gratitude about being a special education teacher, and let that drive deepen and widen professional growth in the future.

_____

_____

_____

_____

Additional Reflections

Important Deadlines

_____

_____

_____

_____

_____

_____

Things to Do in July

_____

_____

_____

_____

_____

_____

_____

_____

_____

_____

_____

_____

_____

_____

_____

_____

FINDING SUMMER RENEWAL

When summer comes, you, as a special educator, have options and choices not available during the traditional school year. This means that you can determine alternative ways to renew your mind, body, and spirit.

Perhaps you have become so familiar with being on the go, working intensively, and often pushing yourself way too hard. Therefore, it could be hard for you to change gear and wind down. Focusing on personal renewal will take time and conscious awareness. Just as you have applied your skill of attentiveness, focusing on the needs of students and families, it is now time for you to be your own case manager. Use these same abilities to determine and prioritize what will benefit you in terms of reviving and renewing your mind, body, and spirit.

Goals

_____

_____

_____

_____

_____

_____

July

July 1

When you have written IEPs, you have created major goal areas such as language arts, math, and behavior. Divide your summer renewal plan into the areas of body, mind, and spirit.

_____

_____

_____

_____

July 2

Give some thought to your fitness status. Think about your weight, strength, and energy level.

_____

_____

_____

_____

July 3

Determine a means to get a fitness evaluation. Feedback from a trainer or friend will give you the basis for a summer workout plan.

_____

_____

_____

_____

July 4

Once you know your work areas, list them under the heading "Body."

_____

_____

_____

_____

July 5

Now that you have work areas, you can look at these as IEP objectives and plan what you need to do in a measurable way by a certain date.

_____

_____

_____

_____

July 6

As you group students for optimal success, consider names of individuals who would be helpful exercise partners for you. Invite them for a walk or a bike ride.

_____

_____

_____

_____

July 7

Be attentive to your eating habits. Are you eating a balanced diet relative to the food groups and your personal needs?

_____

_____

_____

_____

July

July 8

Make a grocery list with your summer eating priorities in mind. Shop wisely with attention to the organic section of your regular store or the features of a food co-op.

_____

_____

_____

_____

July 9

How many hours of sleep had you been getting during the school year? Has this been sufficient? If not, how can you increase your sleep time?

_____

_____

_____

_____

July 10

During the school year, the likelihood of napping was virtually impossible. Now put up the hammock, and vow to use it at least once a week.

_____

_____

_____

_____

July 11

If you live near a beach, go there soon and walk barefoot in the sand. If not, listen to the sounds of waves through earpieces as you walk on a treadmill or in your neighborhood.

_____

_____

_____

_____

July 12

On the "Mind" section of your renewal IEP, list categories of reading material for summer. Perhaps you could divide this into novels, adventures, mysteries, and noneducational informational reading.

_____

_____

_____

_____

July 13

If you have stacked up magazines from the school year, go through them to find something of personal interest to read.

_____

_____

_____

_____

July 14

Take time to participate in a summer workshop relative to your job role *if* you believe that it will reinvigorate your career interests.

_____

_____

_____

_____

July

July 15

If you value journaling, find a quiet and scenic outdoor space to reflect on personal ideas and ideals that have not been addressed because of special education demands.

_____

_____

_____

_____

July 16

Visit your local library to learn about book talks or local lectures. Put one on your calendar.

_____

_____

_____

_____

July 17

After giving and giving as a special educator, you risk depleting your spirit. On the "Spirit" section of your own IEP, list ways that may have occurred.

_____

_____

_____

_____

July 18

Opposite this list of ways you have been depleted, list ways you can replenish that aspect of your spirit.

_____

_____

_____

_____

July 19

During the school year, you have observed student media interests and noted what lifted their spirits or brought them down. Select a DVD or CD to raise your spirits today.

_____

_____

_____

_____

July 20

Attend an outdoor concert. Give yourself permission to be free of hypervigilance and attention to behavior as at school events.

_____

_____

_____

_____

July 21

Pause at various times today to take deep breaths. Look around you and celebrate the freedom from serious responsibility that the moment holds.

_____

_____

_____

_____

July

July 22

Refresh with a new creative project, or pick up one you have begun and left unattended for some time.

_____

_____

_____

_____

July 23

Find a book of daily meditations abandoned because of the heavy focus on work or one new to you. Place the book in a spot where you will read it regularly.

_____

_____

_____

_____

July 24

Assess your spiritual life. How is it different when you are working than it is when you are experiencing less structured times?

_____

_____

_____

_____

July 25

Find ways for gathering with others or taking time out for solitude to enhance your spirituality.

_____

_____

_____

_____

July 26

Learn about the faith expressions of others in your circle. How does this motivate your own growth in spiritual fulfillment and refreshment?

_____

_____

_____

_____

July 27

Find or keep visible symbols and objects to enhance your spirituality.

_____

_____

_____

_____

July 28

Keep attuned to the needs of your body for workouts, healthful food, and rest to counter any cumulative fatigue that may remain from the school year.

_____

_____

_____

_____

July

July 29

Train your mind to be alert to the changes in nature in your immediate environment or its wonders as you travel this summer.

_____

_____

_____

_____

July 30

Special education as a profession demands giving. Find new ways in your family and community to freely give and contribute to the lives of others.

_____

_____

_____

_____

July 31

Resolve to keep all aspects of personal restoration with you through the ebb and flow of life in the days ahead.

_____

_____

_____

_____

Additional Reflections

_____

_____

_____

_____

_____

_____

_____

_____

_____

_____

_____

_____

_____

_____

_____

_____

_____

_____

_____

_____

_____

_____

_____

_____

_____

_____